Janie's Garden

Janie's Garden

Poetry from the Alamo Bay Writers' Workshop 2014

Introduction by Diane Wilson
Lowell Mick White, Editor

ALAMO BAY PRESS
SEADRIFT•AUSTIN

Copyright © 2014 by Alamo Bay Press

All rights reserved. No part of this book may be reproduced in any form without permission in writing from the publisher, except by a reviewer who may quote brief passages in a review.

Photos: Reji Thomas, Pamela Booton, Sophie Rousmaniere
Cover Design: Ironthorn Productions
Book Design: Buffalo Times Productions

For orders and information:
Alamo Bay Press
Pamela Booton, Director
825 W 11th Ste 114
Austin, Texas 78701
pam@alamobaypress.com
www.alamobaypress.com
www.alamobaywritersworkshop.com

Library of Congress Control Number: 2014952502
ISBN: 978-0-9908632-0-5

This book is dedicated to
Janie Waghorne for sharing her magic
garden and to **Lee Meitzen Grue**
for sharing her poetry.

Contents

Diane Wilson
Introduction — 1

Dorothy Barnett
The Swallowtail and the Dill — 4

Linda Caplin
Alfred and the Shrimp Boat — 5

Linda Dane
Birds — 6

Graciela Fleming
In Janie's Garden: An Interactive Site — 7

Lee Meitzen Grue
Janie's Garden — 8

Gina Harlow
Red Headed Stranger — 9

Julie J. Johnson-Jones
Yellow Flowers of Janie's Garden — 10

Diane Kramer
Gardens — 11

Kathryn Lane
   In the Garden of Desire   12

Barbara Williams Lewis
   Stone Mother   14

Bob Lindsey
   Be Patient, My Dear   16

Jay Minton
   She Always Stopped to Pick Up Rocks   17

Aubrey Parker
   The Claw   18

Sophie Rousmaniere
   Janie's Garden   20

Janie Waghorne
   Metamorphosis in the Garden   21

Hazel Ward
   Whimsy   22

Lowell Mick White
   Bear Heads   24

Diane Wilson
   Why I Live in Seadrift   26

   Bios   35

   Acknowledgements   47

   Recent Work by Friends   49

Janie's Garden

Introduction
Diane Wilson

There is a book that I read once that, basically, said our earlier lives prepare us for our destiny. For instance, El Cordobés, the famous Spanish matador, hung around his mother's coattails long past the time that he should because he was preparing himself for the day when he would be in an arena of high danger, boiling red capes, swords, and raging bulls.

Same thing applied with me and my baby sister, Janie, whose garden this book of poems is all about. First thing to remember, though, before I start spouting destiny and her many cards, is that a poem about gardens is more than a book about gardens. It's a poem about the state of one's soul and the poems in *Janie's Garden* book are good indicators of the authors' souls. At least I think so, but don't sue me.

Anyhow, this was how Janie's and my earlier life shaped our souls and pounded our destinies into oyster dust until the fine day came when this little book came out. My little sister and I grew up in a houseful of kids. I was number five and she was number six. We spent a lot of time drawing on the rain cistern. A million gypsies with long black hair and heart shaped faces curving into plunging bosoms and dresses with tasseled ends and on their arms dozens of bracelets, doodads dripping everywhere, and long sharp fingernails with nickel sized ruby rings on at least three, maybe four, fingers.

We did that for years and years until we turned

ten and became missionettes at the First Assembly of God Church. We'd sit around a metal table in an empty part of the church and number paint Jesus' face in oil and eat vanilla wafers and drink red Kool-Aid until our lips were red as a horde of Jezebels. We had a huge responsibility on our little shoulders: just by sitting there we were setting good examples and it was unfortunate that nobody could see us.

When we turned thirteen we were still tomboys. We were country kids, after all! So we would hang by our toes from a high slick chinaberry limb in the front yard to see how long we could stay there until our toes gave out. Sometimes we'd hang ten minutes or so, focusing mightily on our steely toes, then she or I would fall from high in the chinaberry tree. And there we'd be, sprawled in the oyster dust, watching the chinaberry tree watch us, not saying a word cause words ain't necessary when you fall on your head.

When I turned sixteen and my sister Janie turned fifteen, we had a big fight. I can't exactly remember why. I think she said "bra" and I hid under the table in horror, until I finally made my way out and exacted revenge.

In between all these years, we went shrimping with our dad, who I like to call Billy Bones for no other reason than I think it sounds like a pirate.

Anyhow, Billy Bones ran from one bay to the next, steering from a dilapidated captain's chair screwed to the cabin floor with three rusty screws while a handy-dandy-two-burner Coleman stove brewed an eternal pot of black coffee, nearly killing us with the fumes. He was hunting the strange and mysterious hidey holes of shrimp.

Shrimping is hard work but I remember the tiny, tiny details like how we caught a sea horse and a handful of tiny hardheads in that short drag that pulled up nothing else. The hardheads were black and glistening, wetter than rain; newly born babies the size of the tip of my little finger. And the sea horse—one bony sea horse—was the size of a match stick and it died in the deck bucket on the way back home.

I don't think I've said a single thing about *Janie's Garden*.

What was the subject, again?

The Swallowtail and the Dill
Dorothy Barnett

For Janey—Seadrift 2014

Almost in defiance the
green dill thrusts up
reaching for the gray sky.
Here and there, it goes to
seed at the top of the
woody twisted stalks.

This day, it bends low to kiss
the ground as it drops next
season's promise—it
surveys the bay
and the coming storm.

Imagine how thankfully the
yellow and black wings
caress the windblown plant
as the butterfly lays its eggs.

Imagine the weary
swallowtail finding the
heaven that is Janie's
garden—finding the dill
offering a promise of
another season.

Alfred and the Shrimp Boat
Linda B. Caplin

The yellow metal pig with the red wings and blue ears looked up at me hopefully, as if to say "write about me please. Something nice, something happy." What's your name, Piggy? I asked. Well, it's not Piggy, it's Alfred. I said, nice to meet you, Alfred. Tell me, if you didn't live in this part of the garden, where would you like to live? I would love to live on a Shrimp Boat, exclaimed Alfred excitedly! I'd love to go out into the bay with the shrimpers and watch them as they throw out their great nets, then haul their treasure in. I would be good company and not get in anyone's way. Also, if some of the shrimp were too shrimpy or ooky, I would eat them up. The Captain wouldn't have to feed me, and I'd keep the deck clean! I wouldn't have to do this every day, Alfred said, but it would be nice to do at least once. Could you write about that, Lady? I sure could, Alfred, I'd love to!

Birds
Linda Dane

Inspired by a bird in Janie's Garden
"Written on the Fly"

I dream of birds

I dream of cardinals dotting the snow in winter
and squads of pelicans over the bay.

I dream of parrot Charlie Bird kissing my cheek and
murmuring "I love you."

I dream of cranes and flamingos with their long legs
and slow moving grace

I dream of islands of rosy rosetta spoonbills
and summer mockingbird songs.

I want to fly.

In Janie's Garden: An Interactive Site
Graciela Fleming

Tender leaves. Delicate petals.
We go looking for inspiration.
Color galore. Sun and shade.
We go looking for
Something worthy.
Maybe beautiful
Maybe striking
Maybe neither.

Purple leaves densely cling
To a grassy incline
Above the water
Reaching out with perfect strength
Into the rich gulf air.

The breeze in the bay reaches us
Caresses us
Soothes us in summer heat.
Carrying thick moisture
Ahead of delicious rain
It prepares to feed us all
Body and spirit
As we go looking.

Janie's Garden
Lee Meitzen Grue

There are strange gardens—some are stiff and formal—Janie's garden is vivid and lived in. Bright with familiar flowers, rare plants, whimsical artifacts, and the blue pottery of San Miguel de Allende. Although this visitor was aware that there was an immense amount of work done by someone to produce this glorious place, I was only aware after sitting there enjoying it for a few hours, when Janie mentioned her mother planting flowers, that Janie and her mother were the two artists. I later saw a picture of her mother, who has passed, in a big garden hat.

Surrounded by water, this is rich earth for growing flowers and is a fitting tribute. The garden has become a comfortable work of art like a painting you love and live with for a long time. As I sat there musing with the writers of the Alamo Bay Writers' Workshop about the poetry we were writing, I felt more like a happy castaway on some distant island learning a new culture and a new language with a group of friends, and no tourists.

Red Headed Stranger
Gina Harlow

Prone, naked, and rusted
she strikes a pose.
Her conceited gaze etched
in veins pulled from the earth.
But she is not of the earth.
She looks not at you, but to the water.
She lies, soft curves, harsh to touch.
But she does not want you to touch.
She sits as stone, waiting to return to the sea.

Yellow Flowers of Janie's Garden
Julie J. Johnson-Jones

Pink Roses, Purple Violet Smells, Green Grasses
Sculpted Like by Hand

Bushes, Shrubs, Grasses and Stone.

All Are Beautiful, but then I Stop…

In Front of The House, Down by the Bay,
I Found My Peace.

I Found Yellow Flowers, Blowing in the Wind.

It Makes Me Think of the Yellow Roses Given to
My Grandmother,

It Reminds Me of My Michigan Husband Giving Me
"Yellow Roses of Texas" because of a
Song He Heard.

But Most Of All, Yellow Flowers
Light Me from within,
Just Like a Warm Summer Day at the Lake, and
This Brings Me Joy.

Gardens
Diane Kramer

Janie's garden nestles beside her home,
    perched at the edge of the continent.

Cultivated paths of stepping stones wind
    in and about, past orange and red and
    pink flowers,

Green grass and myriad browns of
    soil and sand resist the salt soaked air.

Statues stand proud and guard her handiwork,
    never tiring.

Just beyond, lives God's garden.

Carved by ancient seas, the harbor yields to the
    waters of the bay where bands of gray travel
    to the blue crown of the universe.

Herons and egrets fly toward the clouds,
    sending ripples across the water.

Lanterns of moon and stars hang in the night sky,
    sentinels to all below.

In the Garden of Desire
Kathryn Lane

I walked in a garden, hibiscus,
flowering azaleas and Mexican bird
of paradise, and I saw a hand,
not the hand of God, for that I saw
in much larger gardens—Bruce, Zion,
Grand Canyon and Monument Valley,
but this garden had a simple hand
with curled fingers, working fingers.

What is the meaning of finding
a hand in a garden? I thought
of immense possibilities, universal
ideas sparked by those gnarled
knuckles; memories of Michelangelo
sculpting the Pietà, or sleek, modern
fingertips tapping keyboards to reach out
and find someone to ease existential pain.

Words—spoken in the same garden
by a woman seeking to find herself,
a woman lucky enough to grow up
in a loving family yet who never met
her biological parents—her words echoed
in my mind. Why are we so compelled
to find our roots, and in searching, we feel
it will fulfill our emotional needs and desires,

thinking it will center us, like plants
spreading roots to anchor themselves
in the soil, flourishing in rain, withstanding
violent windstorms, or like giant Saguaros
storing precious moisture in their pleated spines
to survive desert droughts. When plants find
rejection, do they curl up and die, or do they
sprout more underground tendrils?

The hand in the garden, basking in the sun
on sunny days and bearing the cold in winter,
appears content, not asking where it came from,
not questioning its origin but merely lying there,
uncovered, unprotected, without hidden meanings,
without secrets, allegorically providing a guiding
hand, a helping hand to azaleas, hibiscus and delicate
Mexican bird of paradise flowers.

As thinking, emotional beings, we question
why the universe exists and why we are here,
and lose ourselves in sorrow, not knowing
answers to what we seek. In rejection, each one
of us handles it as best we can, yet I ask
if adopted people ever think that some of us
who grew up with bio-parents, if given a choice,
might have chosen to be adopted.

Stone Mother
Barbara Williams Lewis

There is a mask in Janie's garden.
A symbol of fertility.
She sits stone-faced
At the edge of the pavilion.
Her back is to the water.
She is surrounded by lilies:
Plantains, tigers, I think,
And lovely tall grasses.

Her back is to the horizon on purpose.
She draws in the power of the water
To nurture Janie's garden.
She absorbs the energy
To share with her sisters.
She attracts those
Who would pass her.
With a blind eye
She makes them see.

Without softness
She is tender.
Without light
She brings joy.
She has no hair, no teeth,
Yet she is complete.
She has learned to be
Bigger than trauma.

If you bring your troubles to her
She utters no sound.
She, alas, speaks to your soul
In ways no other has done.

I call her Stone Mother.
Perhaps I should call her Mother Stone.
She told me that I cannot fix what is broken
If I continue to use the tools that broke it.

Stone Mother. Mother Stone.
Jasper, Hematite, Unakite, Jade,
Obsidian, Pearl, Ruby, Diamond.
These are her sisters.
Like the daughters of Zeus and Mnemosyne
They all have healing powers.
It is Mother Stone, however,
The Stone Mother
Who gives them directive.

Be Patient, My Dear
Bob Lindsey

The fig peeked past
fat leaves, so called foliage,
same as covered Adam and Eve,
the low hanging fruit, still green
full of promise for a patient
gardener.

"Wait until I'm ripe," whispered
the fig—"then pick me!"
But I pushed past, onward
to the apple orchard.

She Always Stopped to Pick up Rocks
Jay Minton

She always stopped to pick up rocks. Often, way too many of them. So, I suggested starfish. She thought that was a great idea. It only took her a few minutes to realize there weren't any just lying around. With a sideways glance, she went back to picking up rocks again. I started to talk about sea glass and how cool and smooth it is. She once again started to look for the latest suggestion from Mr. Smarty Pants, but soon realized sea glass was also virtually non-existent on this beach. Her bag was so full now, it was almost dragging on the ground. I smiled at her struggle, but knew better than to say anything. They were her rocks, fair and square. She asked if I wanted to go home. I said "No….not just yet. Let's check out this next cove."

As we came around the large set of rocks at the point, we saw them. Hundreds of them, maybe thousands. She just looked at me and shook her head. Our eyes locked in terror. Was this some experiment gone wrong? Maybe some kind of volcanic underwater eruption? Unknown. I laughed weakly and kidded her, "Well, there you go. There's some starfish for ya." She joked back and said "Sure, but what did you have in mind for sea glass?"

The Claw
Aubrey Parker

Ode and Owed to a Rusty Twisted Garden Tool in Janie's Garden

He ruled the garden with an iron claw.

No one in the garden could match the ruthlessness of his reign of terror.

Any upstart was severely ripped from its roots and cast aside to wither away in the heat of the Sun.

One-two, one-two, his vorpal fingers strangled the life of many a foe.

Little did he know his reign could never last.

He never realized that his mortal enemy would be the very sodium chloride that brought life to others.

As he lay dying in the sand,

His once bright fingers twisted and tarnished,

His last thoughts were visions of Rustoleum and WD-40.

He was cast aside to die
    while the Dandy Lions snickered at his pain.

Janie's Garden
Sophie Rousmaniere

It was quiet and still in the garden
Save the whirring of inspired minds
Pens writing on paper with vigor
The most visceral words they would find

The words spoke of flowers and trees and small pigs
The chicken scratch handwriting flattered small twigs
Janie's garden delighted, inspired and cleared
The minds of the Alamo Bay writers there.

Thanks, Janie, for a lovely visit!

Metamorphosis in the Garden
Janie Waghorne

Black and neon green caterpillar on dill slowly
    crawls, eating, changing.
So still, yet transforming right before my eyes.
You blend, like I, so the world cannot see you.
Busy, busy as you eat and grow, then becoming
Ever so carefully your own tomb, the chrysalis.
You wait and wait for your secret to reveal—the
    lovely wings to unfold.

Whimsy
Hazel Ward

I am planted here in this garden
of perfect fits…
lush sweet potato vines flow around me
green carpet pillows for the humble bee.
Purple wisteria float and float
To where I cannot see…
My neighbors' world in dappled light.

All are fragrant,
brilliant colored hues
I am not.

What am I?

A pumpkin yellow pig stuck to the ground.
Body rotund.
A snout that will never learn to root…
Too tiny and Rubenesque.
I am the indecorous decoration
Discreet and still.

Why cast me, a misfit,
At the curved edge?

An iridescent butterfly hovers,
Spying my red tipped wings
Drops down, down

Hovers uncertainly
Then sharply flies away...
I resemble no butterfly,
graceless, pushed low to the ground,
unspread wings that cannot fly.
Pigs would not own me either...
What pig has blue ears, stuck too high?
I can neither slide nor glide,
nor fly...
can perform no feat of daring,
only sit and mark a spot.
My place in a garden ill defined
Incongrous, but yet it's mine!

Bear Heads
Lowell Mick White

Page Ware sold Sunoco gasoline,
ran a store for forty-seven years.
He kept the heads of four
black bears mounted on the walls
of the store.

He lost most of a forefinger fixing
a fanbelt, and he would jab
the stump at me when he spoke:
"Now, you see I *know.*"

He jabbed, talked,
sold gasoline and soda pop, sold
canned spaghetti and potato chips,
talked, told stories, sold aspirin,
shotgun shells, frozen hamburger,
white bread, recommended
cures for diarrhea and poison ivy,
sold hunting licenses and
bologna, detergent and
ice cream and he gave
free advice.

The bear heads on the wall listened
to him and the old grizzled men
who hung around the store
listened to him, too. Even I listened to him,

sometimes. Of course Page didn't *know*
anything, really, but he was never a
man ashamed of things he didn't know.

When I finally went home
I asked about him, at dinner.
My aunt said, "Why, poor old Page's
been dead these three years." And
I blinked.

I looked out the window,
down the road.

I wondered
what happened to those
bear heads.

Why I Live in Seadrift
Diane Wilson

I freely admit that I have spirit eyes. I can see the bay as an old grandmother with long gray hair and a dress made of matted foaming seaweed flowing out with the tide. I imagine that black drum nibble on her dress more than they nibble on the oyster spawn growing in the oyster reefs.

This grandmother is pretty particular. She doesn't like name-calling or measuring tools of any sort. For instance, a compass or Loran readings or a GPS or a measuring tape can't locate the position of her left foot or how far her hair trails out to sea. It just takes a bend in the right corner of my mind and there she is clear as rain on new tin.

She's certainly as real as my other physical-as-a-doorknob grandma who takes me to the bay with her to head shrimp. Only I'm not heading shrimp and making a dollar for Jesus like Grandma is doing. Oh no! While the other women stand around a big wooden table and pinch the heads off of shrimp the live long day, I'm looking through the cracks in the wharf for the water lady.

I know this water woman. I know where she lives. I taste her briny bones on my tongue and when a storm or a hurricane approaches the town, the front row seat in the Church of Jesus Loves You can't beat her for pure, unadulterated, unmitigated razzmatazz.

I am anchored in Seadrift near a very salty sea

where there is intuition excluding rationality, dreams excluding language, and mysteries excluding a clanking, cranky world. I am a borderline mystic, a tad unsociable, and happy as a clam.

Janie's Garden

Janie's Garden

Janie's Garden

Bios

DOROTHY ELLIS BARNETT dropped out of high school, took the GED, and entered college in her mid-thities. While in her forties, she graduated from The University of Texas at Austin with a BA in Anthropology, an MA in English, and a James A. Michener Fellowship. She is professor emerita in English and Creative Writing at Austin Community College, where she taught for over 20 years. She earned an MFA from Pacific Lutheran University in her sixties while conquering breast cancer. Additionally, she was a founder of *Borderlands: Texas Poetry Review*, *The Rio Review*, and the anthology for the Poetry Festival at Round Top where she was one of the founders of the festival.

PAMELA BOOTON is a longtime Austin resident who is active as an arts advocate and financial consultant. She serves as founding director of the Alamo Bay Writers' Workshop and publisher of the anthology *ABWW13*. Pamela was co-editor of *The Amazing Imagination Vacation*, project manager for the oral history documentary *Seadrift Fishermen Legacy Project*, and the organizer of the Texas Louisiana Gulf Coast Shindig. She is a consultant for the Reji Thomas studio, Graphic Glass Studio, and Pine Street Station. She is also a consultant for the Mos Chukma Institute, which provides art therapy to children at the Dr. Martin Luther King, Jr. School in the Lower Ninth Ward of New Orleans.

Pamela is an associate producer of the documentary *Radio Taboo* and promotes performances by artist/activist Issa Nyaphaga, providing community radio to Cameroon, West Africa. She is a member of Impact Austin and the Austin Documentary Fans and serves on the board of *Issue TV*. She is an active promoter of the writing of Lowell Mick White and the glorious art of Reji Thomas. Pamela lives in Austin with her husband Javier VanWisse and their two dachshunds, Rudy and Grady.

LINDA CAPLIN is writing her memoir of a life full of adventure and joy. From her travels as a Peace Corps Volunteer in Ecuador to a career as a counselor at Austin Community College, and now to reflection by the pool with kids, grandkids and four legged kids, Linda shares a life well lived.

After a corporate career in Dallas, LINDA DANE has retired to the beautiful coastal town of Palo Alto. Linda spends her time writing, reading, and pondering the orangest sunrises in Texas.

GRACIE FLEMING spent her childhood in a place where the land turns from desert to ranch and farmland and springs feed a beautiful river that Mexicans call Bravo and Americans call Grande. It is something of an oasis where locals keep secrets, travelers trade stories, and magic abounds. Those stories, secrets, and magic color the novels, stories and poetry she writes. She lives in Austin where three deeply gratifying commitments nurture her writing. She is part of a creative community known as Alleywriters. She serves on the advisory council for Alma de Mujer Center for Social Change. She is married to her dearest friend.

LEE MEITZEN GRUE is a highly acclaimed New Orleans poet and fiction writer, whose work celebrates New Orleans culture and music. Her published books include *Trains and Other Intrusions: Poems*; *French Quarter Poems*; *In the Sweet Balance of the Flesh*; *Goodbye, Silver, Silver Cloud*; and *Downtown*. As a Visiting Writer, she has conducted seminars and performed her work at La Universidad de Barcelona in Spain; at Librairie, an English language bookstore in Paris; at Westminster College in Fulton, Missouri; and at the University of Hawai'i at Manoa international symposium "The Literature of Place." The recipient of an NEA Fellowship, with prizes in poetry and fiction from Deep South Writers, The Associated Writing Programs, and a PEN Syndicated Fiction Prize, Lee has taught at Tulane University, Westminster College, and Xavier University. She is the former Director of The New Orleans Poetry Forum and The First Backyard

Poetry Theater and is long time editor of The New Laurel Review. Renowned Civil Rights activist, Lee was a founding member of the renowned Quorum Club, which integrated the French Quarter and was the New Orleans hub for the Freedom Riders throughout the '60s. She owns the celebrated and beloved bar BJ's Bywater, home to many of New Orleans music royalty. Her novel Blood Root will be published in the coming year.

GINA HARLOW: I'm a native of California and have lived in Austin, Texas, for 31 years. Currently, my husband and I plus two grand-doggers reside on an old horse farm, (minus the horses—used to be horses—that's the book!) on two acres at Lake Travis. I have two beautiful grown children that have abandoned me for lives of their own, if you can imagine. I am the co-author of a recipe column with Angela Shelf Medearis, *The Kitchen Diva!* that is syndicated nationally through Hearst, King Features. I also author my own blog *Peaches and Prosciutto* about food and gardening. I am currently working on a memoir. When I'm not writing, gardening and cooking I'm sailing on Lake Travis.

I am JULIE JEAN-MARIE JEWERT JOHNSON-JONES. I have been married to a wonderful man, Charles Jones, for 10 years. I have 5 kids and 5 grandbabies. I am celebrating the 7th anniversary of my 40's on July 4th. I was given up for adoption 40 plus years ago, and given to this WONDERFUL FAMILY that I share with my brother Jason. I am a Mexican/Puerto Rican/Black mixed woman, and have spent most of my life trying to figure out Who I am? Why my parents do not have a great tan like me? How can I help others like me? and figuring out life. My father Russ gave me the skills to build, plan & organize. I watched his dad build furniture and toys, just like I watched my dad build furniture and all kind of cool outdoor things. So whenever I get a chance to play outside making things I do. Benches, Tables, Catios & Planters sets. My love of wood is as important as my love for Fabrics and Writing. This comes from my Grandma Jean & Mom Linda. I make quilts, clothes, purses, Bags & Halloween costumes. But the writing…well that's an inside hobby just waiting to break out. I just want to be able to write down everything I think about or go through, and maybe someday be able to help someone with my words. Touch someone the way so many wonderful people have touched me in my past.

DIANE KRAMER is a retired community college counselor from Austin, Texas. She is working on a collection of essays about the kindnesses that people do for others called Humanity Rides the Bus; her entry "A Rolling

Community" won honorable mention in a contest sponsored by Capital Metro in 2011. She also writes about social justice issues and her article "Different Eyes" appeared in the September 2012 issue of the online journal Social Justice Today. Her letters to the editor have been published in the Austin American Statesman, Dallas Morning News, Texas Observer, Time, and the Wall Street Journal. Diane is a guest blogger on the web site for Peace Through Pie www.peacethroughpie.org.

KATHRYN LANE writes both fiction and poetry. Her short stories have been published in *New Border Voices: An Anthology*; *Swirl Literary Journal*; *Arriba Baseball!*, and *ABWW13: the Alamo Bay Writers' Workshop Anthology*. Originally from Mexico, her writing is often inspired by Latin American cultures, and she performs poetry in both English and Spanish. Kathryn's poems have appeared in the *Austin International Poetry Festival Anthology (*2012, 2013 and 2014 editions); *Homeless Diamond*s, a London-based journal; *Primitive Archer*; *Swirl Literary Journal* and *Poetry at Round Top Anthology*. She has two chapbooks of poetry, *A Conversation on India* and *Spirit Rocks*. The Friendswood Public Library featured her poems when their blog showcased the Rothko Chapel and Mark Rothko's art.

Dr. Barbara Lewis is Professor of English and Assistant Dean of Academic Departments at Austin Community College. She received her PhD from University of Southern California. Proud mother of four, grandmother of thirteen, and great grandmother of seventeen, Dr. Lewis lives near Austin, Texas. Dr. Lewis recently published the first volume of her memoir, *Sherrod Village*. She is working on her autobiography, *Reflections of a Woman Wild*.

Bobby Lindsey was born in Seadrift, Texas; graduated from Midwestern State University; owned a private investigation agency in Dallas; was a field producer for NBC News in Europe; was Baseball Coach at International High School Frankfurt, Germany; was International Scout for the Cincinnati Reds baseball team. Presently, he is retired in Seadrift, Texas. He has had poems published in local newspapers.

Jay Minton is a passionate sound designer, composer, musican, art director, web designer and Jack of all trades. He has worked as a production sound recordist in Thailand, Bali, Cambodia, and all over the US. He is a prop maker and art director, creating specific pieces to fit the needs of each production. Jay's sound work is extensive, creating foley effects, playing a wide variety of instruments and creating the emotional lubricant that only good sound can do.

AUBREY PARKER is a painter, sculptor, and songwriter from Bexar County, Texas. Growing up on a farm near San Antonio with only dairy cattle for company, Parker humorously claims his social skills were learned from cows. The exploration of painting, sculpting, writing songs and poetry has defined Aubrey's life. His career has ranged from joining the Coast Guard after college, to twenty years as an Electronics Field Engineer for RCA, to a college teacher of electronics and computer technology, to serving his country in the Coast Guard Auxiliary. Aubrey's retirement home is on Keller Bay in Olivia, Texas, where he remains active in the arts and community. Aubrey builds and rides motorcycles, restores old cars and is the manager and curator of the Seadrift Art Boat.

SOPHIE ROUSMANIERE has worked as a filmmaker and freelance journalist in the US, Canada, India, Indonesia, Mexico, Guatemala, Pakistan, Laos, Vietnam and Thailand. She has produced, edited and directed over thirty documentaries, short films and music videos. Sophie's work is largely social issue based, having worked on topics from child prostitution in Thailand to environmental issues in the Four Corners area in New Mexico. She is currently wrapping up a documentary slated for broadcast on PBS: *Yellow Fever—The Navajo Uranium Legacy*. Sophie is Executive Director of Issue Television, a non-profit media organization for education.

The art of **Reji Thomas** spans the range of grand paintings on canvas to architectural embellishment pieces to photography to monumental glasswork. Reji's acclaimed art work, in private collections and in public places, is cherished by many around the world. Clients include the State Capitol of Texas Restorations, Democratic National Convention, Ann Richards, Barbara Jordan, B.B. King, corporate headquarters and colleges and universities throughout the Austin area, the Rotary Club, Human Rights Commission, Holy Angels Catholic Church in San Angelo, the Mayor's Office of the City of Austin, gifts from the Texas Governor's Office to the President of Mexico and the Queen of England, to name just a few. Reji has owned and operated Eastside art hub Graphic Glass Studio and music venue Pine Street Station since 1979. Pine Street has hosted the Fader Fort venue during SXSW, featuring such music greats as Amy Winehouse and Kanye West. Pine Street Station has also been a longstanding and key part of EAST (East Austin Studio Tour). Reji Thomas continues to support Austin creativity and to produce brilliant art.

JANIE WAGHORNE, retired teacher, community leader, and mother, hosted the Alamo Bay Writers' Workshop, Seadrift 2014 poetry class of Lee Meitzen Grue in her magic garden on San Antonio Bay. Janie's Seadrift roots run deep, back through generations of fishermen and a family of educators and writers. Janie and husband Steve host many family gatherings for siblings, children, the growing number of grandchildren, and friends. Janie has carried forward the finest traditions of community heritage with her leadership in the Seadrift Centennial, the Seadrift Fishermen Celebration and the Legacy Project. Janie has been a leader in education, from her years in the classroom to contributions to book clubs to world travels. She graciously shares some of her own writing with our friends of Alamo Bay.

Born in the small town of Plaquemine, Louisiana, DR. HAZEL WARD is the recipient of numerous awards and honors, including the Woodrow Wilson fellowship and a Ford Foundation grant. The literary and academic community has certainly benefited from her numerous highly respected publications and presentations. Dr. Ward has taught English at colleges and universities throughout the Austin and Houston area. Her career has taken her from Professor to Dean of Communications at Austin Community College. Dr. Ward is the ultimate educator, poet, writer and humanist. We are fortunate to have Dr. Ward as our moderator.

LOWELL MICK WHITE is the author two novels, *Professed* and *That Demon Life*, and of the story collection *Long Time Ago Good*. A recipient of the Dobie Paisano Fellowship, Mick graduated from The University of Texas, and then earned his PhD at Texas A&M University. He has been a NEA resident writer teaching creative writing at the federal prison for women in Bryan, Texas, and presently teaches at Pittsburg State University. Mick is a member of the Alamo Bay Group, featured instructor of fiction for Alamo Bay Writers' Workshop, Editor-in-Chief of the Alamo Bay Press, and editor of the ABWW anthologies. He is now working on a new novel set in his home state of West Virginia. Mick is a member of the Texas Institute of Letters.

The author of *An Unreasonable Woman*, DIANE WILSON, is a fourth-generation shrimper who began fishing the bays off the Texas Gulf Coast when she was eight. By twenty-four she was a boat captain. While running her brother's fish house at the docks and mending nets, she read a newspaper article that listed her home of Calhoun County as the number one toxic polluter in the country. She set up a meeting in the town hall to discuss what the chemical plants were doing to the bays. Diane claims that in everyone's life they will encounter a piece of important information and what they do with that information will determine the course of the rest of their life. And so began her life as an environmental activist. Her fight for the environment and for justice has won her a number of awards: *National Fisherman Magazine* Award, *Mother Jones*'s Hell Raiser of the Month, Lois Gibbs' Environmental Lifetime Award, Louisiana Environmental Action (LEAN) Environmental Award, Giraffe Project, Jenifer Altman Award, Blue Planet Award, and the Bioneers Award. Co-founder of Code Pink and the Texas Jail Project, Diane continues to lead the fight for social justice. In pursuit of justice and protection of our environment, Diane's travels have taken her to Bhopal, Beirut, Baghdad and back to Seadrift. Her acclaimed writing captures the imagination and the conscience of us all.

Acknowledgements

Alamo Bay Writers' Workshop
    May 30-June 1, 2014
    Seadrift, Texas
    www.alamobaywritersworkshop

Alamo Bay Group
    Pamela Booton, Director
    Lowell Mick White, Editor
    Diane Wilson, Freedom Fighter

Instructors
    Diane Wilson
    Lowell Mick White
    Lee Meitzen Grue

Moderator
    Dr. Hazel Ward

Featured Readings
    Dr. Barbara Williams Lewis, *Sherrod Village*
    Dorothy Ellis Barnett, *Road Songs*

Photographers
    Sophie Rousmaniere, Filmmaker
    Reji Thomas, Artist

Lodging
Captain's Quarters—Seadrift

Class Venues
Captain's Quarters
Janie Waghorne, Janie's Garden
The Harbor

Dining
Bubba Hall, Bubba's Cajun Seafood
Rocky's Noodle House
La Terraza
Picnic at Pavillion, City of Seadrift

Art Center Seadrift
Aubrey Parker, the Art Boat

Printer
Dana Burton, D&J Blueline Printing

Consultant
Pat Taylor, Artist

Alamo Bay Press
Lowell Mick White, Editor-in-Chief
Diane Wilson, Associate Editor
Pamela Booton, Associate Editor

Recent Work by Friends

ROAD SONGS, by DOROTHY ELLIS BARNETT. In a mosaic of beautifully crafted lyric essays about a childhood on the road, Dorothy Ellis Barnett takes us from the humid riverbeds and campgrounds of the East Texas piney woods to the busy trailer courts of Southern California, across highways and blacktops, and the Formica tabletops where her adopted father, Kenneth, teaches her to flip dominoes and count playing cards before she is eight years old....

SHERROD VILLAGE, by DR. BARBARA WILLIAMS LEWIS. In 1982, Barbara Williams Lewis became a thirty-seven year old runaway when she moved to Los Angeles with her three children. Born black and poor in Wilson, North Carolina, Lewis chronicles the events of her life that led to her self-imposed exile and her struggles to go beyond it, She tells her story with honesty, humor and raw emotion. She speaks freely of her mistakes and her political views about money, religion, rape, incest, corruption and domestic violence, and she shows her ability so triumph over poverty, homelessness and pain.

PROFESSED, by LOWELL MICK WHITE. *Professed* is a novel filled with the struggles and rivalries and oddities and weirdnesses of contemporary American higher education—yet as the characters strive to fit into a rapidly changing institution, medicating themselves as best they can with sex and drugs and literature, learning actually happens. Somehow....

IRONTHORN PRODUCTIONS is an Austin-based company working to develop compelling film, video and marketing content for writers, artists and forward-thinking businesses. Want to make a video about your upcoming book? Adapt your short story into a short film? Promote your work online? Contact Ironthorn Productions.
SOPHIE ROUSMANIERE & JAY MINTON
ironthorn@hotmail.com
www.ironthorn.net

www.alamobaywritersworkshop.com

www.ingramcontent.com/pod-product-compliance
Lightning Source LLC
Chambersburg PA
CBHW072109290426
44110CB00014B/1876